Practicing Kwanzaa Year Round

Affirmations and Activities
Around the Seven Principles

by Gwynelle Dismukes

G
SUMMERTOWN, TENNESSEE

© 2000 Gwynelle Dismukes

Cover Design: Gwynelle Dismukes,
              Warren Jefferson
Interior Design: Gwynelle Dismukes

Published in the United States by
GlobalCultures Ink
Book Publishing Company
P.O. Box 99
Summertown, TN 38483
888-260-8458
www.bookpubco.com

ISBN: 1-57067-113-3
Library of Congress #00-192135

Contents

Introduction 4

The Nguzo Saba.............................6

What is Kwanzaa? 7

Why Kwanzaa Year Round? 10

The Affirmations 13

The Adinkra Symbols 14

The Activities.................................16

Umoja...20

Kujichagulia...................................26

Ujima 34

Ujamaa 40

Nia 46

Kuumba 52

Imani 58

INTRODUCTION

From the time I first started leading Kwanzaa workshops and presentations in the early '90s, I have had my audiences doing most of the work. They set the Kwanzaa table as I explain the various items, they read the Principles, and they participate in group singing and dancing. I believe this is one reason for the success of these presentations with a range of age groups from preschoolers to seniors. People enjoy being included and having a chance to take an active part in what is going on. Inclusiveness is one of the primary characteristics of African culture, in which each person is valued and respected as a member of the community of all living things that come from the same Creator.

Another aspect of Kwanzaa which I feel has particular appeal with adult audiences is the rich symbolism and meaning found in the Seven Principles, the items on the Kwanzaa table, and the ceremony of lighting the candles. The progression of technology in Western culture has sent an increasing number of people searching for ways to make their lives more grounded and more meaningful. The culture of Africa offers a wealth of moral, spiritual and psychological benefits because of its profound sense of communalism and affirmation of life.

These two aspects of Kwanzaa—inclusiveness and meaning—can be tremendously helpful for character development, self-esteem, and spiritual growth. For this reason, I am sharing with readers some of the exercises and activities I have used with audiences over the years, or practices I and others have participated in, such as the susu and the Kwanzaa altar.

When Kwanzaa was first adopted by socially active African Americans in the early '70s, it proved to be an effective organizing and teaching tool, instilling a sense of identity and self-confidence in young black children. I believe we have only begun to explore the ways in which Kwanzaa can be used to invigorate and strengthen individuals, families, communities, and ultimately our whole society.

I hope this book will encourage more people to start *today* to bring a deeper spirit of this wonderful holiday into their lives.

Gwynelle Dismukes

THE NGUZO SABA

Umoja/Unity
To strive for and maintain unity in the family,
community, race and nation.

Kujichagulia/ Self-determination
To define ourselves, create for ourselves,
and speak for ourselves.

Ujima/Collective Work & Responsibility
To build and keep our community together; to make
our brothers' and sisters' problems our problems,
and to solve them together.

Ujamaa/Cooperative Economics
To build and manage our own stores, shops and
other businesses and to profit from them together.

Nia/Purpose
To make as our collective vocation the building
and developing of our community in order to restore
our people to their traditional greatness.

Kuumba/Creativity
To do always as much as we can in the way
we can in order to leave our community more
beautiful and beneficial than we inherited it.

Imani/Faith
To believe with all our heart in our parents,
our teachers, our leaders, our people, and the
righteousness and victory of our struggle.

WHAT IS KWANZAA?

Around a large table covered with red, green
and gold cloth, a group of men, women and
children are gathered in joyful anticipation.
The women wear brightly colored skirts and
blouses, their hair braided in intricate styles or
covered by yards of wrapped fabric. The men
and children are dressed in the loose style and
boldly patterned garments of a distant continent. On the table are ears of dried corn, fresh
fruits, vegetables, and a wooden cup, all rest-
ing on a large straw mat. Arranged in a pyra-
mid-shaped candleholder are seven candles.
As the ceremony begins, candles are lit and
strange words are spoken, with the children
helping to carry out each activity.

This scene occurs in many households in
the U.S. and around the world during the last
week in December, as families observe the
African American holiday of Kwanzaa.

Developed by cultural activist Maulana
Karenga and others during the Black Consciousness movement of the 60s, Kwanzaa
serves as an affirmation of positive ethnic val-

ues and identity during a traditionally European, gift-oriented holiday season.

Taken from a Swahili word meaning "First Fruits," Kwanzaa is based on the African celebration of the harvest, when the village collectively gives thanks and celebrates the rewards of its labors. The American adaptation of the tradition emphasizes familial and communal efforts and cooperation, and reinforces positive values for the African American community as a whole.

In their creation of a new black holiday, Karenga and his committee sought to improve the self-image of African Americans by presenting strong African role models, strengthen the African American family through activities in which all family members participate, and unite the African American community in the shared observance of a cultural tradition that is uniquely ours.

Kwanzaa is structured around the Nguzo Saba, or Seven Principles, which are still the foundation of many Afrocentric schools and community re-education programs aimed at black self-awareness and empowerment.

Kwanzaa lasts seven days, one for each of the principles, and applies practical interpretations to traditional elements of African culture, reinforcing the moral concepts of the holiday.

The observance of Kwanzaa occurs from December 26 to January 1 and involves preparing a table with the mkeka, kinara and mishumaa saba, muhindi, kikombe, mazao, and zawadi. Each day a candle is lit, representing a different principle. The principle is explained and examples given, often in story form by the children. An African folktale may be read or a story may be told about an outstanding African or African American figure.

The seventh day of Kwanzaa is an occasion for families to gather together in a communal celebration. African songs are sung, there is drumming and dancing, and zawadi are exchanged, as the community completes its thanksgiving and prepares to move joyfully into an even more bountiful new year.

WHY KWANZAA
YEAR ROUND?

Each December many of us dust off the kinara, bring out the mkeka, and get ready for the karamu in celebration of Kwanzaa. But does any of this make a difference in our lives from January to November? Or have the Seven Principles become a mere cultural formality?

I suggest that the Nguzo Saba can be a vehicle for personal and collective empowerment and a way to deal with our present crises as individuals and as a people. If we are to bring about a real change in our present condition, we must begin to utilize moral and spiritual resources such as the Seven Principles to ground and direct us through the social confusion of our times. If the Nguzo Saba are to mean anything to us at all, then they must become living principles, honored and followed in our daily lives. Our Kwanzaa tables should remain up all year long, to serve as a focal point for our energies and a reminder of our commitment to our personal goals and ideals and to the progress of our people.

Perhaps most important, we need to establish a personal relationship with the Seven Principles, one which allows them to become an intimate part of our being. The Nguzo Saba are based on universal principles applicable in all times to all people. If we further personalize them to our individual philosophies of living, we can focus their energy into a laser beam of clarity and strength which can create the conditions for positive change, manifested at all levels of our daily existence.

In order for the Nguzo Saba to become an active part of our lives, they need to be constantly reinterpreted to address the issues of our changing and progressing social condition. This book presents a more personal interpretation of the Nguzo Saba, drawing upon the universal aspect of the principles. This gives the Nguzo Saba a broader application for the individual, both in terms of his/her own growth and development, and also in terms of his/her relationship to the various communities of which we are all a part.

We are also introducing the use of traditional Adinkra symbols from Ghana as a means of graphically illustrating the seven principles. Through fresh interpretations and the use of ancient symbolism, we seek to expand the concept of Kwanzaa so that it may become a more powerful moral guiding force in today's African American community and the world.

To help readers make Kwanzaa a more active part of their lives, we are adding activities for each of the principles to show how these ideas can be demonstrated in the midst of our daily routine or group gatherings.

There are at least seven key values that are part of traditional African culture:

∞ caring for the children
∞ honoring the elders
∞ respect for all life
∞ partnership with the earth
∞ reverence for the ancestors
∞ active relationship with the spirit world
∞ responsibility to the community

These values are reflected in the *African Values Pledge*, included as one of the Ujima activities in this book.

THE AFFIRMATIONS

An affirmation is a statement of something which we wish to see manifest in our lives. It is a positive statement of our intention which serves to motivate, inspire, and move us toward our goals. By verbally affirming a condition or way of being, we acknowledge that it already exists in potential, and it is only a matter of time before we are able to see it in our present reality.

Frequently repeating the affirmation to ourselves reinforces our ideals and desires, and builds up faith in our ability to realize our dreams. We can create affirmations for anything in our life that we want to change or create. The more personal the affirmation, the more powerful it is.

The affirmations in this book are intended merely as examples of ways in which we can incorporate the positive qualities of Kwanzaa in our ongoing work of self-improvement. Each person is urged to develop their own personal statement of the Seven Principles as they apply specifically to their own goals and ideals.

The Adinkra Symbols

Since the beginning of history, man has used symbols to communicate not only with his fellow human beings, but also with the higher, unseen forces of the universe. The power of the symbol lies in its ability to directly affect the subconscious in conveying its message.

Symbols play an important role in the establishment and maintenance of community. They serve as a visible representation of identity, shared knowledge, and common experience. Through symbols, individuals can be persuaded to commit to something greater than themselves, and the realization of a collective goal becomes a primary motivating force in the life of every member of the group.

Not only are symbols important to the group, but they can also be a powerful tool for the individual. The symbol serves as a focal point for the energies of the person using it, returning and reinforcing those energies in a continual loop of psycho-spiritual interaction. Thus, the conscious understanding and application of symbols can be an effective tool for personal and collective empowerment.

Throughout Africa the use of symbolism is pervasive. Designs carved or painted on furniture, utensils, clothing, and buildings serve far more than a decorative function; they may tell a story, illustrate a proverb, or help to create and maintain an energetic field around the area or object.

The traditional Adinkra symbols are patterns stamped on cloth primarily by the Asante people of Ghana in a process developed sometime around the 19th century. Adinkra cloths were originally worn only for mourning or other spiritually oriented ceremonies. Today, however, in the city streets of Ghana one sees Adinkra symbols on everything from buses to handbags to wooden stools to jewelry.

Because of their wide and increasing popularity, we have chosen seven of the sixty-four traditional Adinkra symbols to represent the Seven Principles of Kwanzaa.

Just as the Nguzo Saba are based on universal principles, the African symbols also express primary concepts shared by people of all cultures. Each person is free to develop their own unique relationship with the symbol, based on their own intuitive response to it.

THE ACTIVITIES

Any job, skill or talent we have must be developed through practice. As with our outer physical abilities, so too with our inner, personal abilities. Every day we have an opportunity to put forth our best effort to be tolerant, to be honest, to be balanced, to be self-confident, to be more or less of whatever we want to be in accordance with our highest vision of ourselves. Any adjustment of our personality toward the perfection of our character can be accomplished by finding actions that echo our highest ideals and putting them into practice. Sometimes these actions may be symbolic representations of higher concepts and principles.

Traditional African culture recognizes the value of process; that is, experience is considered more valuable than theorizing. In Western culture, we are often told what we need to do but not how to do it; we may grasp the concept of some principle of behavior, but do not know how to bring it into practical manifestation in our day-to-day affairs.

In this book we offer activities designed to represent and put into practice the Seven Principles of Kwanzaa. Some are gathering activities that are enjoyable community-building exercises for families, classrooms, church and social groups, and youth programs. Other exercises encourage individuals to look inside themselves and examine their own attitudes, emotions, and ideals, and suggest ways to put those ideals into practice in the course of ordinary life.

Through these activities, groups and individuals can physically demonstrate the various principles, reinforcing their effectiveness not only for themselves, but for others who may also wish to participate. Ultimately, we hope to stimulate the inclusion of the Seven Principles on a deeper level in our lives throughout the year, so that their influence can be seen in our ennobled and empowered thoughts, words, and actions every day.

TRADITIONAL
SYMBOLS OF KWANZAA

Mkeka The straw mat, representing tradition as the foundation of the family and community

Kinara The seven-stick candleholder, representing family background

Mishumaa Saba Seven candles: 3 red, 3 green, 1 black, representing the Nguzo Saba or Seven Principles

Muhindi Ears of corn, representing the children of the family

Kikombe Unity cup, representing interdependence

Mazao Basket of fruit, symbolizing the rewards of labor and blessing of abundance

Zawadi Gifts for the children, a reward and recognition of their hard work and contributions to the family during the previous year

Karamu The communal feast usually held on the last day of Kwanzaa

The Seven Principles

In this section each principle is presented in three ways:

The Adinkra Symbol

On the left is the Swahili name for the principle, and an explanation and interpretation of the symbol. On the right is the name of the principle and the corresponding Adinkra symbol with the Ghanaian name underneath.

The Affirmation

On the left is the name of the principle in Swahili and English and an interpretation of the principle in personal terms. On the right is a suggested affirmation for the principle.

The Activity

The suggested activity for each principle is given on these pages.

UMOJA

The name of this symbol translates
literally as "Bite not each other"
and represents justice, peace,
unity, and harmony.
It reminds us to be as forgiving and
compassionate as possible with one
another, in the interest of living
peacefully together as brothers and
sisters of one human family.

Unity

Bi Nka Bi

Umoja

Unity

According to the traditional African
perspective, every living thing comes
from the same Spiritual Source, and
therefore everyone and everything is
equally deserving of respect.

When we have the realization that all
Life is One, we begin to open our hearts
to others and we receive blessings in
return. We can see that it is in **our** best
interest to hold the best interest of **all** at
heart. We understand that what we do to
another, we do to ourselves, and so we
are always careful in our relations to
respect all Life.

*May I become more aware
each day of the Oneness of the
universe. May I be less selfish
and more serving of the
Greater Good, of which I am
a small, but important part,
along with every other
Living Thing.*

Umoja Activity

HARAMBEE CIRCLE

This is a group activity that works well as a closing for meetings and programs, and as a gathering activity for cultural celebrations. It is rousing and energetic, and helps pull the group energy together.

All participants should gather in a circle holding hands. The group then calls out together, "Harambee" seven times, each time raising their hands in the air. The last time, the group should extend the last symbol and make it a good, long shout. Harambee (pronounced hah-rom-bay) is a Swahili word that means "let's pull together."

As a variation, the Harambee circle can be used to send positive energies to other groups on the planet. Someone in the circle could begin by saying, "Let's pull together for all the children." The group responds by raising their hands together and saying "Harambee!" The leader or other members of the circle in turn may call out someone or something else to pull for, followed by the circle's response. The group may pull together for the children, the elders, the ancestors, for those who died in the Middle Passage, for those unable to physically be in the circle, for all living things on the planet, for the seven generations to come, and for any others that the group may wish to include. (It's just important for someone to keep count of the Harambees so you know when you get to seven!)

KUJICHAGULIA

This symbol represents patience, self-containment, self-discipline, and self-control. Without these things, we cannot grow to be responsible, well-balanced, and productive members of our family and our community. These qualities, along with honesty and respect for all living things, are essential to the development of our character and help to determine the course of our lives, positive or negative, in this lifetime.

Self-Determination

ANI BERE A ENSO GYA

KUJICHAGULIA

SELF-DETERMINATION

Rites of passage and initiation
ceremonies in traditional African
culture place a great deal of emphasis
on self-discipline as a means of
attaining personal power and realizing
one's full potential. Self-discipline and
self-expression are the twin keys to a
balanced, effective, and productive
character.

Let me seek, find, and maintain
that balance of freedom and
control that allows me to fulfill
my destiny in this life.
Let me always act from my
Highest Self and respond to the
promptings of Spirit within me.

Kujichagulia Activity

BOTH SIDES

This is an individual activity which can be repeated at intervals to help people become aware of their personal resources in shaping their lives.

For best results, the first time you do this activity you should stop as soon as you read step 1 and do that part of the exercise. Read step 2 and do that part. Then read step 3 and complete the exercise. This way, you won't influence your responses and you may be more surprised at the results. (Of course this requires self-control and self-discipline, represented by Ani Bere. Good luck!)

STEP 1

Get a large sheet of paper and fold it in half. On one side of the paper, list your personal strengths, qualities, and experience in terms of your character or in terms of a particular issue that you may want to address in your life at the time. For example, if you are feeling like your social life needs adjusting, write down what makes you a good friend, parent, child, sister, coworker, husband/wife, etc. Think of talents and traits that are helpful or important to your dealings with others. Or, if you are doing a general exercise, think about what you appreciate most about yourself. (This first step in itself is a good exercise in self-affirmation!)

To combine Kuumba in this exercise, use markers or crayons to decorate your sheet or draw pictures to represent your ideas. Or write your ideas at different angles in different colors. Be creative!

STEP 2

On the other side of the paper, write down things you want more of, areas that you would like to improve. Think of what your real needs are, and be as specific as you can. For example, if you want a better job, what about the job do you want to be better, what personal need do you want to have satisfied? If you want to be more patient, how do see that helping you? Evaluate yourself and your needs as honestly as you can so that you are not distracted by superficial desires.

Before you go on to step 3, stop for a moment and take a couple of deep breaths. Remind yourself that you have the power to determine what you will do with the resources given to you in this life. Let your chest swell with satisfaction as you review the positive things you wrote about yourself in step 1. Consider that with all you have done, you can do more, and feel the energy of your self-confidence growing with your deep breaths. After a few moments of this and when you feel ready, go on to step 3.

STEP 3

Open the sheet and look at both sides. In all probability, you will find some thing or things on the first side of your sheet that can directly help you to achieve something on the second side. Think about the relationships between the first list and the second list, and see what that tells you about what is going on in your life.

To combine Imani in this exercise, put your paper on the Kwanzaa altar when you are finished, to symbolize a spiritual partnership in realizing your potential.

UJIMA

Shaped to represent an enclosed and secured compound house, this is a symbol of safety and security, brotherhood and solidarity. It reminds us of the inner sense of security that comes from being a valued and respected part of our communities.

Collective Work
& Responsibility

FIHANKRA

Ujima

Collective Work & Responsibility

We are all, by nature or by choice, members of a number of different social groups, from our racial and sexual orientation to our family of birth, to our church, workplace, or social group.

Our membership benefits us and the group in many ways, and it also involves responsibility:

(1) for each of us to be responsible for ourselves as far as possible (the strength of a community is based on the strength of its members);

(2) for all of us to be responsible to and nurture our various communities so that they in turn can nurture us.

Let me all ways, as well as I can, recognize and fulfill my responsibility to myself and to those around me.

May I find strength in the performance of my duty, and may that strength be increased by sharing it with the members of all my communities.

Ujima Activity

WORLD IN OUR HANDS

This is a group activity that reminds us of our responsibility as human stewards of the planet to care for all the different people and things living on the planet with us.

Participants should gather in a circle and pass a globe or other round object around the circle while singing this song.

Most people know the song, "He's got the whole world in his hands." For this variation, the chorus is, "WE'VE got the whole world in OUR hands." Some of the verses might be:

"We've got the little bitty babies.. *in our hands...*"

"We've got the grandmas and the granddads..."

"We've got the birds and the animals..."

"We've got the rivers and the trees..."

"We've got the past and the future..."

Participants should suggest other variations in the verses as they feel inspired.

AFRICAN VALUES PLEDGE

We join together—
    to care for the children,
    to honor the elders,
    in reverence for the sacred,
    with respect for all life,
    in partnership with the earth,
    with the guidance of the ancestors,
    and with deep appreciation of our
        cultural heritage,

We join together—
    to uphold the Seven Principles in
        our daily lives,
    and to support one another in
        working for the Highest Good
    for ourselves, our families,
        and our community.

UJAMAA

This symbol depicts two crocodiles
sharing a common stomach. They
illustrate the fact that we are all
interdependent, and our success—in
fact, our life—depends upon all of us
working together for our mutual benefit.

Cooperative Economics

FUNTUMMIREKU
DENKYEMIREKU

Ujamaa

Sharing

"What goes around, comes around."
This expression is a common one in the
African American community, but in its
most positive sense it refers directly to
the concept of Ujamaa. What we share
of our resources—whether time, talent,
money or energy—returns to us as
additional resources through which we
can creatively improve our situation and
progress toward our individual and
collective goals.

*May I generously give of all
that I have to those who
need it, and may I be open
to receive and utilize the
resources and opportunities
which come to me in return.*

Ujamaa Activity

SUSU

This activity requires a year-long financial commitment from a small group of people who decide to circulate their resources in the group in some specified amount. The susu is an established social institution in Nigeria.

One way to form a susu is to get 12 people who each agree to put in, say, $10 a month. In January, 11 people send $10 to the first person in the group. Next month, 11 people send $10 each to the second person in the group. The person who receives money in a month does not pay anything that month. In this way, each person gets $110 once a year. Often this money comes at just the time when it is needed. Or people can make plans in advance to use the money they will get when their month rolls around. If participants choose their birth month, as close as possible, then the money comes as a birthday gift!

In today's busy world it may be necessary to simply send the money on a specified date, but a pleasant variation would be for the group to actually meet once a month (or quarterly) and present their gift for the month in person. Having the occasion be a potluck lunch or dinner would be a way to even further promote community and sharing.

This plan can be adapted in any number of ways, but it requires a firm commitment from all the members in order for it to work. If someone is chronically late sending their gift or drops out halfway, it just ruins the whole thing. On the other hand, this activity can be a way for people to look at their feelings around friendship and money, and to deal with some of the issues that may come up for them. Without question, the need for balance in our material, emotional, and spiritual relationships with others, with ourselves, and with the earth is one of the greatest challenges of our technological times.

NIA

This symbol and its name have become
well known through the movie called
"Sankofa" and through numerous
African American artistic and
commercial uses of the word. Literally,
it means, "It is never too late to go back
and fetch what has been lost."
It has been used to encourage African
Americans to "go back" and reclaim our
past, our heritage, and our ancient
African wisdom. Through the
knowledge of our past, we can gain
a greater understanding of our purpose
in the present and our destiny
as individuals and as a people.

Purpose

SANKOFA

Nia

Purpose

The act of being responsible demonstrates that a person is committed to a certain standard of behavior. Through commitment to an ideal, to a goal, to a positive, ongoing relationship with someone or something, we find our purpose in life and begin to fulfill our human potential.

*May I have an increased
understanding of my purpose
in life, and may all my
energies be constantly
directed to that end.
May I take full advantage of
every opportunity to develop
my human potential for love,
service and fulfillment.*

Nia Activity

SETTING INTENT

In the rush and press of everyday concerns we can easily forget our intentions to be kind, to reserve judgment, to follow our highest instincts in all things. So it is important to set our intention at the very beginning of the day, while we are still fresh from the physical and spiritual renewal of sleep, and preferably before our consciousness is distracted by other voices. A visual representation of this intention can be helpful to recall during the course of the day when we need to refocus.

You can use the Sankofa symbol as just such a reminder. First draw a copy of the symbol, as large or small as you want, on a sheet of paper. In the middle, write your heart's intention; whether it is to gain knowledge, to spread love, to give assistance, etc. It is good to take some time in quiet to narrow down exactly what is your intention at any given time in life, in order to practice what is sometimes called "reaching the core of one's intent." You want to state your goal as concisely and honestly as possible.

Then, starting at the top of the heart on either side you choose, write along the outline of the symbol what the effects of this goal or intention would be in your life. For example, if your goal is to give assistance where needed, you might say that the person you help will be less lonely. Or if your intention is to be more assertive, then the effect might be that others respect you more and therefore are able to benefit from what you have to offer. If your goal is to gain knowledge, the effect might be that you gain better control of your emotions and become more effective in your daily life.

Whatever you write, follow the curve of the symbol, reminding you when you look at it, that the effects in your life are the result of causes, i.e. choices, which are largely determined by you. Then every morning look at your symbol, and use it to remember your goals and the positive and desirable effects of achieving them.

KUUMBA

Depicting a snake climbing a raffia
palm, this symbol represents ingenuity,
excellence, and performance of great
feats. Observing the most ordinary
details of Nature has inspired poets,
musicians, philosophers, and scientists
to make wonderful creations,
inventions, and discoveries. We too can
be inspired to new ways of thinking
simply by paying attention to the
natural world around us.

Creativity

OWO FORO ADOBE

KUUMBA

CREATIVITY

Finding a new approach to something—
innovation—requires independent
thinking and the ability to apply
information in a creative way.
By thinking for ourselves and allowing
for the process of discovery, it becomes
possible for us to conceive and create a
new reality.

Open my mind to new ideas and ways of living. Let me bring to each possibility my own unique creativity, and produce from it something which expresses the essence of who I am.

Kuumba Activity
KUUMBA ROOM

This is a guided visualization designed to help people open up to creative possibilities. It can be used for an individual meditation or can be done with a group by someone familiar with relaxation techniques.

Sit comfortably in a quiet place where you can be free from distraction for about 10-15 minutes. Take a few deep breaths, as long and slow as possible, and focus your attention on your breathing, allowing yourself to be fully aware of all the sensations involved with the air coming into your body and circulating through your system. Let your muscles relax until you are totally free from tension anywhere in your body.

When you have reached this point, allow yourself to imagine that you are going to your Kuumba Room. This is where you can create anything you want without any limitation or restriction whatsoever. It does not have to be a room, it can be anywhere, and whatever you need in order to create is there for you. Let your imagination go wherever it wants, don't hold back, remembering that you are in your own private world where you are in complete control and can change the picture you are seeing at any time. Enjoy the feeling of freedom in creating with no restriction.

As you complete your creation, tell yourself that you are going to find ways to continue to have this wonderful feeling in your life, that you will be more creative in your daily expression and in your environment. Let your attention slowly return to your body and your breath, and gradually open your eyes and stretch, as you would after a short nap. If you get any fabulous ideas while in your meditative state, be sure to jot them down so you don't forget them before going on to other business.

IMANI

One of the most important and
meaningful of the Adinkra symbols,
Gye Nyame is simply translated,
"Except God." One interpretation is,
"No one has seen this world from its
beginning and no one will see its end—
except God." It is symbolic of the Spirit
within each of us, through which we
can elevate ourselves to a new level of
consciousness and self-actualization.

Faith

GYE NYAME

IMANI

FAITH

"This far by faith." The faith of our
Mothers and Fathers—Martin,
Malcolm, Sojourner Truth—was not in
images or doctrines, but in a personal
relationship with a force that was
greater than themselves and yet was
also within them. We each need to
develop and strengthen our personal
relationship with whatever we hold as a
higher power in our lives, calling upon
the great spiritual heritage of our
mother continent to invigorate and
sustain us in all aspects of our being.

*The power I need in order to do
great things comes from spiritual
connectedness. Let this be the
groundwork for all that I think
and all that I do in this physical
plane. Let me nurture a close
relationship with my Higher
Power, the ancestors, and the
positive spiritual forces
of the universe.*

Imani Activity
KWANZAA ALTAR

Whether you celebrate Kwanzaa alone or as part of a family or group, you will undoubtedly be involved in setting up a Kwanzaa table. You or your group can make the Kwanzaa table an energy center and a focal point for honoring the sacred in your life and expressing reverence for ancestors and spiritual helpers.

An altar is basically a sacred space, set apart for people to communicate with the unseen forces of the universe. In the traditional African village setting there are usually numerous shrines to various spirit guardians throughout the community. In their own homes, people also have a space set aside to honor the ancestors, those departed members of the family whose memory and spirit are kept alive through the devotion of their relatives here on earth.

To use the Kwanzaa table as an altar, it must be dedicated to that purpose and not have any other miscellaneous objects on it.

Anything that goes on the table must have some special energy or significance. If used to honor the ancestors, photographs or other memorabilia may be placed on the altar. Fresh fruit and/or flowers can be placed on the altar, particularly during special occasions.

The Kwanzaa altar can be a place for the group to gather for a moment of silence, prayer, or reading the African Values Pledge before meeting or beginning an activity. It can be a place to bring the group together when there is a need for reuniting and refocusing energies. It can be a place where individuals can contemplate their spiritual growth and communicate with their higher power.

The principles of Nia and Imani can be combined when the altar is used to assist people in making changes in their lives. Write the goal, intention, need, or affirmation on a piece of paper and place it on the altar, or find some object that represents the goal to put on the altar. Using the Kwanzaa table in this way combines positive cultural and spiritual forces in a visible form that helps to support our intentions and efforts to realize our full human potential.

To schedule a workshop, presentation, or speaking engagement by Gwynelle, see contact information below. Also see our complete catalog of Native American titles and vegetarian cookbooks.

Book Publishing Company
PO Box 99
Summertown, TN 38483
931-964-3571
Fax: 931-964-3518

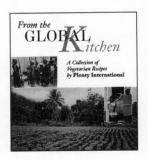

Orders: Toll-Free
888-260-8458

website:
www.bookpubco.com

e-mail:
bookpubl@usit.net